Implementing Strategic Fluff

HOW TO TURN STRATEGIC CONCEPTS INTO ACTIONABLE STRATEGY

A Workbook for Making Strategic Fluff Real

Bill Welter

MindPrep Resource Center

2019

Implementing Strategic Fluff

MindPrep Resource Center

Loveland, Colorado

Copyright © 2019 by Bill Welter

All right reserved, including the right to reproduce this book or portions thereof in any form whatsoever. For information, address

MindPrep Resource Center

1733 Monarch Circle

Loveland, CO 80538

Implementing Strategic Fluff

CONTENTS

INTRODUCTION	1
WORKBOOK OBJECTIVES	1
Workbook Structure	2
But first, some ground rules	4
PART 1: THE BIG PICTURE	5
Step 1: Answer this question	5
What is your organization's strategy?	5
Factors affecting your strategy	6
Pacing factors: they are out of your control	6
deeper Responses to pacing factors:	7
Ten factors that you can control (to some degree)	9
Changes	9
Step 2: Look at your functional silos and your strategy. What should you change?	10
Factors driving your strategy:	10
Driving Factors	10
Enabling Factors	12
A problem to consider and resolve	19
Strategy Factors Matrix	20
Step 3: get ready to work cross-functionally	22
PART 2: BUSINESS ECOSYSTEM and competitor INTELLIGENCE	24
Step 4: Think about your business environment	24
Step 4 (cont'd): Answer these questions about your ecosystem.	29
Step 5: Consider your competitors.	30
Step 5 (cont'd): Answer these questions	34
PART 3: think cross-functionally	35
Step 6: Consider all the necessary changes	36
one on one relationships	37

Implementing Strategic Fluff

Step 6 (cont'd): Answer these questions	52
PART 4: BRINGING IT ALL TOGETHER	53
Step 7: Summarize the situation	53
Step 8: Think like a project / program leader	56
PROJECT LEADERSHIP CHECKLIST	56

My thanks to Richard Rumelt

Professor Rumelt published *Good Strategy / Bad Strategy: The Difference and Why it Matters* in 2011. In this wonderful book he enumerated the four hallmarks of bad strategy. They are:

- Fluff
- Failure to face the challenge
- Mistaking goals for strategy
- Bad strategic objectives.

His opening explanation of *fluff* is "Fluff is a form of gibberish masquerading as strategic concepts or arguments. …. apparently esoteric concepts to create the illusion of high-level thinking."

Shortly after reading his book I had a discussion with VP of marketing for a rather large firm and when I asked him about the company's strategy to grow, he said it was "simple – to delight our customers!" Rumelt's explanation of fluff popped into my head. It's been there ever since.

INTRODUCTION

Too many business strategies are expressed as fluff or fiction. This situation is not new – we've been fooling ourselves for decades. We think we can discover "the secret" to strategic success and bypass complexity by focusing solely on the supposed secret. We try to make strategy seems simple and straightforward. It's not.

In the 1970s we were convinced that Japanese companies would take over the world with their emphasis on quality. We thought we could simply send legions of middle managers to Japan to copy their tools and techniques. But it wasn't the tools and techniques as much as the culture of quality and the relationship between management and the workforce that made the Japanese different.

During much of the 1980s we watched manufacturing companies try to create "the factory of the future" by focusing on technology. We installed systems and robots and manufacturing cells; but we often neglected to consider their impact of the workforce. General Motors spent a fortune on automation technology – and failed.

In the 1990's we were overcome with short-term thinking masquerading as brilliant insight. The wisdom at the time was to compensate executives with stock options so that they would take a longer-term view of the company and improve its performance steadily over time. But this incentive scheme fell prey to the reality of people gaming the system to make the stock worth more in the short term. Stock appreciation became more important than company success.

In the early years of this century we became enamored with the concept of becoming "lean and mean." We've been trying to starve ourselves into prosperity while we're trying to embrace innovation as our latest savior of business. But the culture of lean and mean abhors waste while the culture of innovation embraces experimentation (and the waste that goes along with it.) The truth is that if we want innovation, we must accept some _inefficiency_!

As we approach the quarter-century mark, we are both enamored with and frightened of the "gig economy." On the one hand we are seeing innovation and risk-taking. On the other hand, we are seeing people trying the "hope is a strategy" strategy. A few will succeed wildly; but many are forfeiting their future. Also, while many people cheer the low unemployment numbers, we have wage stagnation and the near-elimination of the vaunted "middle class" lifestyle of the mid-twentieth century.

WORKBOOK OBJECTIVES

Strategy is never simple; it's complicated at best and often complex. The work involved with executing strategy is even more so. It's downright messy.

This workbook was developed for those managers and professionals who are involved with the development and execution of strategy. These are the people who are expected to "make strategy

Implementing Strategic Fluff

real" in their organizations and have no choice but to deal with the messiness behind the simple statements.

These managers and professionals will not be asked to develop the high level (corporate) strategy but they may be asked for input. And whether or not they have input to the strategy they will be expected to understand it and apply it at their level for their department or team.

Therefore, there are a few overarching objectives to this workbook. After using (not just reading) this workbook a manager should be ready to:

- Discuss the business strategy with the boss and ask meaningful questions about the competition and the business environment.
- Explain the business strategy to her/his team in terms that they understand.
- Translate the business strategy into actions that should be taken to implement the strategy.
- Discuss the ripple effect of the strategy across the organization.

WORKBOOK STRUCTURE

Developing and executing strategy should seemingly be rather straightforward :::: but it's not. For some strange reason, we manage to consistently mess up a logical (but not simplistic) process. That's why I wrote this workbook.

Look at the following matrix and decide where you and your team need to spend some quality thinking time.

It would be great if	But :::	So, you should ::::
You quickly notice meaningful changes in the business environment.	Sometimes you are so busy dealing with day-to-day issues that you are unaware of subtle, or not-so-subtle, changes in the business environment.	Dedicate time to examine competitor and business environment changes. Use Part 1 of this workbook. I've provided an approach you may want to consider. If you don't like it, build one for your specific situation.
These changes cause you to rethink the goals of your organization.	Sometimes you don't (re)define our business goals or you don't make them clear to the workforce.	Ask your boss (or your boss' boss) about organizational goals. Don't let them off the hook until they explain it in ways you can understand. (Goals are outside the scope of this book)

Implementing Strategic Fluff

It would be great if	But ...	So, you should ....
Modified goals mean you modified your business strategy. This triggers the need for a "big picture" change.	Sometimes you don't know what to change. AND Sometimes you don't know what else will or has to change.	Get specific about what has to change. Concepts and metaphors are not enough! In **Part 2** I'll explain the twelve factors that pace, drive, and enable your strategy. In **Part 3** I'll provide a way to think about interrelationships among these factors.
This strategy results in a portfolio of projects that will be used to execute the strategy.	Sometimes you don't have the capabilities or capacity to execute the portfolio of projects. Prioritizing projects may be difficult due to competing beliefs about what will yield the best results.	Work hard to keep intention and execution in balance. **Part 4** will provide comments and suggestions.

This workbook

I'm not offering a simple solution to executing your organization's strategy. I am suggesting an approach to thinking about the work you have to undertake if you want your strategy to succeed. The value in this workbook comes from working through the questions I've posed.

This workbook is divided into four parts.

- **Part 1: The Big Picture** addresses the problem of stating strategy in general or conceptual terms and introduces twelve factors you must consider as you try to make your strategy real. To start, you should answer the following question:
  - What IS our strategy? Can you explain it clearly?
- **Part 2: Competitor and Business Intelligence** explains the two factors that set the pace of change for your strategy. These are the rate of societal and industry evolution (often referred to as your "ecosystem,") and changes your competitors make. I will give you a quick way to explore both business intelligence and competitor intelligence. If you are going to make strategy real you must be prepared to answer two additional questions:
  - What's changing, and what is the source of these changes?
  - How fast is the change taking place?
- **Part 3: Integrate Your Thinking** digs into ten factors that make up your business strategy. Two of these factors (customers and offerings) drive your strategy. The other

3

eight factors are used to enable your strategy. Develop answers to the following questions:
- What should we change?
- What can we change? (Are we resource constrained?)
- What will we change? (Will our culture allow needed changes?)
- What else will or must change?

- Finally, in **Part 4: Bringing it All Together** I will give you a process to follow to use these factors to assess your current situation and prepare for the future. You will need to answer the following question:
  - What are the technical, organizational, and behavioral challenges we must overcome?

BUT FIRST, SOME GROUND RULES

Making strategy real depends on your willingness to adhere to a few simple rules:

- You and your organization (company, hospital, firm, not-for-profit, etc.) are not alone. You are simply a part of much larger system. Accordingly, you must be willing to think about the ecosystem in which you operate. Recognize the power of context.

- Strategy without the ability to execute it is simply wishful thinking and a waste of time. Don't think about strategy and then think about execution. Think about them iteratively. Keep intention and execution in rough balance. Consider tradeoffs.

- Be brutally honest about the predictability, malleability and harshness of the industry in which you operate now and will operate in the future. Do you need to be big, or first, or fast in order to succeed? Will the things that got you to today get you to tomorrow? Be brutally honest with yourself.

- Experts know that change is needed. Concepts and generalities have a nice sound, but they are just words. Convert your strategic concepts into "strategic specifics." Focus on things you should change.

Implementing Strategic Fluff

PART 1: THE BIG PICTURE

What do "world class," "customer delight," "unparalleled quality" and "operational excellence" have in common? How about the executive challenge of "let me give you a stretch goal!"

They are all ideas that exist in someone's mind – but are not real in the sense of knowing what must change. The CEO does not have a dial on her desk that she can move from 1 to 10 and magically improve business results. The Marketing VP cannot change quality by declaring it so, and the VP of Operations can't flip an "excellence" switch.

Moving these concepts from someone's mind to perceived reality requires changing real things in the real world. A hospital doesn't become world class because it says it is. It becomes world class by hiring superb doctors and nurses, adhering to "never-event" procedures, and learning from the industry's success and failures.

A business becomes world class by creating, developing, hiring and inventing better ways. Apple is not just another consumer electronics company. The Mayo Clinic is not just another hospital. And Amazon is not just another e-commerce company. They are different and they are different in very specific ways.

STEP 1: ANSWER THIS QUESTION

Answer the following question in writing. Seriously, write the answer. If you can't, it's likely you don't know the answer. And, please, avoid jargon.

WHAT IS YOUR ORGANIZATION'S STRATEGY?

Remember, strategy always answers the question "How will we succeed?" Use your own words to answer this question.

Did you provide a general or a specific answer? The more specific the better. **Remember, you can't execute what you don't understand. Get clarity!**

FACTORS AFFECTING YOUR STRATEGY

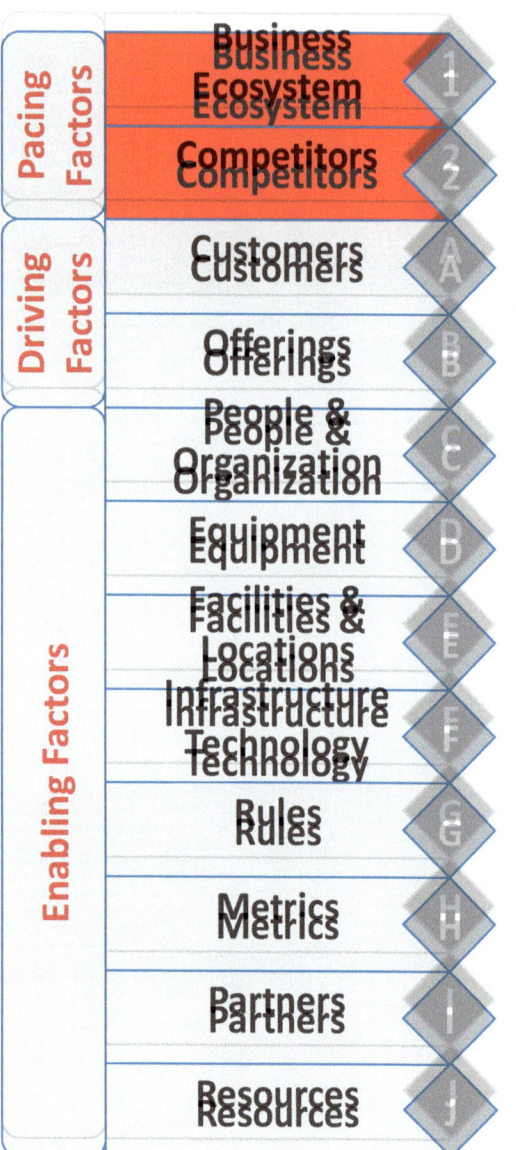

There are twelve factors that will determine the success of your strategy. Two are out of your control and you have varying degrees of control over the other ten.

PACING FACTORS: THEY ARE OUT OF YOUR CONTROL

No matter how powerful you think your organization is, there are two factors outside your control that will set the pace for developing, modifying or executing your business strategy:

1. Business ecosystem (the industry and social setting in which you operate):

2. Competitors (current and emerging)

Implementing Strategic Fluff

DEEPER RESPONSES TO PACING FACTORS:

Since the two factors are out of your control, you must watch them and, hopefully, respond in time. I've provided a few suggestions for responding to the context factors and a question for you to consider:

1. **Business ecosystem:** Think bigger than your industry, especially if you are a B2B company. What is happening politically and societally? How are demographics changing the competitive landscape? Are Gen Z customers acting and reacting like your Gen Y customers? As you come to understand your business ecosystem, here are a few ways in which you might act. Which one might describe your organization?

Ignore ecosystem changes and continue on your proven path of success.
"Intercept the future" and change your business model to appeal to future customers and an evolving environment.
Watch and wait for significant problems or opportunities.
Question: What are you doing (and more importantly, going to do) about your changing ecosystem?

Implementing Strategic Fluff

2. Competitors: Who's going after your customers and whose customers are you trying to capture? When you consider your existing and newly evolving competitors there are three common responses. Which response do you see your organization?

	Ignore them. (You do this at your peril, especially new or different competitors.)
	Match them move for move. Let them set the tone for the industry.
	Preempt them. Move before they get a chance to take advantage of your competitive stance.

Question: What are you going to do about your competitors? Summarize your competitive strategy.

Implementing Strategic Fluff

TEN FACTORS THAT YOU CAN CONTROL (TO SOME DEGREE)

In general, there are ten factors that an organization can use to gain and maintain (if only for a short time) competitive advantage. The factors are:

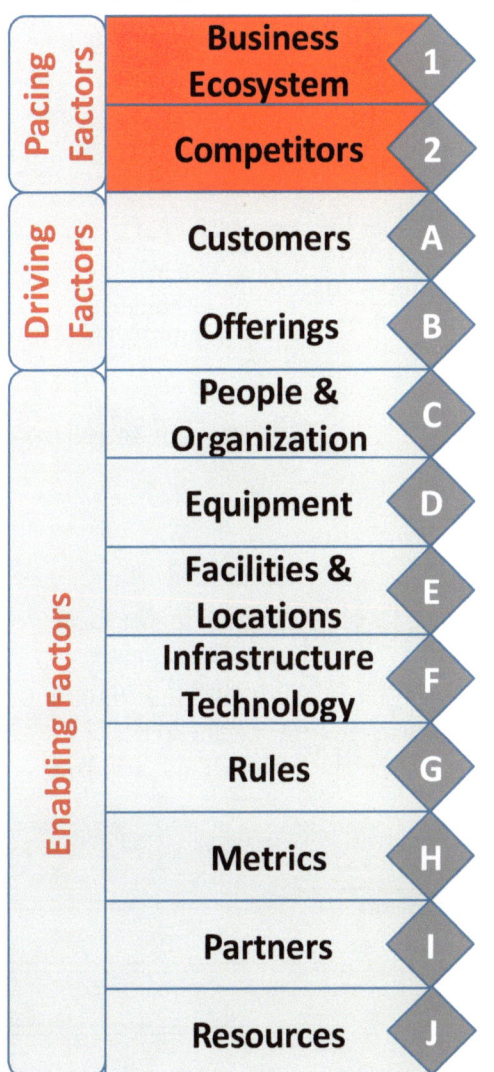

A. **Consumers and customers**: the people who use your offerings and the people who pay for this use
B. **Offerings**: the products and services you provide
C. **People and organization**: the people who work for you and how you organize their talent
D. **Equipment**: the machinery and systems used to produce your offerings
E. **Facilities & Location**: buildings, geography, layout, use of space
F. **Infrastructure technology**: information systems, operating systems, etc.
G. **Rules**: business and departmental policies, procedures and "ways of doing things"
H. **Metrics**: measures of success and progress
I. **Partners**: suppliers, professional support services
J. **Resources**: money, information, know-how, facilities

Different C-level and department executives have responsibility and decision rights over all of these. Although lower level managers have limited decision rights, they always have the responsibility to influence the executives to modify these factors for the good of the organization.

CHANGES

Strategy development and implementation always includes the need to understand changes in context and to bring about change within your organization. Your de facto strategy is seen in the changes you are making.

STEP 2: LOOK AT YOUR FUNCTIONAL SILOS AND YOUR STRATEGY. WHAT **SHOULD** YOU CHANGE?

Either you will respond to competitive forces coming from outside your organization or you will initiate internal change to succeed over competitors. This means that somewhere along the way you must change one or more of your strategy factors or try to influence someone who can.

FACTORS DRIVING YOUR STRATEGY:

Although Competitors and the Ecosystem will set the pace of strategic change, two of the factors within your control will drive your specific strategy: Customers and Offering. You may decide to follow your customers wherever they lead you, or you may decide to lead your customers by offering new products or services. Once you have a handle on this issue, the rest of the factors are used to enable your strategy.

I've provided a few suggestions for responding to each of the factors and a question for you to consider. Note that this is not an exhaustive list.

DRIVING FACTORS

A. **Customers and Consumers**: You will accept money from anyone who buys your product or service. But there is a more important question: Who do you <u>want</u> as a customer? For whom will you spend time, effort and money to have them come to you? Here are some actions you can take. Check which of these will help you modify your current strategy.

Keep some or all our existing customers.	
Attract and add new customers.	
Drop unwanted customers.	
Treat some of them differently from others.	
Question: Who are your <u>target</u> customers and what are you going to do for them?	

Implementing Strategic Fluff

B. **Offerings:** What products and services do you offer that customers are willing to purchase? What do customers want that you are not offering? Why? Here are some things you can do to modify your offerings strategy.

	Create new products and/or services. These could either be new to you or new to the world. Watch Amazon continue to disrupt the entire retail industry while offering the same products but doing business in a different way
	Drop existing offerings. This may be difficult if you have a "heritage" product or service.
	Improve your offerings. "Newer and better" may be an old move, but it still works. Consider the regular upgrades to Apple's iPhone.
	Make your offerings different from the competitors' offerings in ways that appeal to customers.

Question: Do you need to change your offerings as you look into the future? Short term? Long term?

Implementing Strategic Fluff

ENABLING FACTORS

Now we're getting into changes that take place at the departmental and functional levels. Fluffy grand strategy must inevitably become specific Here are eight factors.

C. People and organization: Do you have the talent needed to produce the offerings your customers will want in the future? Are you organized in ways that customers and the workforce appreciate? Think about some of the changes available to you.

	Hire talented people. (Why not hire the best people? Too expensive?)
	Fire those workers who damage your chances of success.
	Relocate the workforce geographically or virtually.
	Develop workers and leaders to meet and exceed needed skills.
	Reorganize work effort. Combine departments. Outsource.
Do you have the right talent and organization needed to serve future customers with profitable offerings?	

D. Equipment: Production equipment converts tangible and intangible assets to viable products and services. Think about some of the changes available to you.

	Upgrade equipment to state of the art
	Upgrade equipment state of the market
	Institute preventive and predictive maintenance programs
	Replace human labor with robots and machines
	Replace fixed-use machinery with multi-purpose machinery

Is your equipment both effective and efficient for the emerging products and services demanded by your customers?

Implementing Strategic Fluff

E. Facilities & Location: Do you need special-purpose facilities such as high-rise warehouses or cyber-secure buildings? Are you in the right location? Big-picture location moves include opening operations in a different country or region. Detailed location moves include a change to a lab layout. Here are a few things to consider re: facilities and location

Build, lease, rent	
Stay where you are or leave a country or region or city	
Move entire operation to a different location or move equipment within an existing space.	
Open a new location.	
Question: Is everything where you need it to be to serve your customers? Do all your current locations contribute to your success?	

Implementing Strategic Fluff

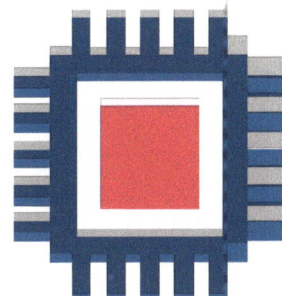

F. Infrastructure Technology: Infrastructure technology is the collection of techniques, skills, methods and processes used by your business to produce your products and services.

	Acquire evolving and state-of-art technology.
	Develop proprietary technology.
	Abandon old and obsolete ways of operating.
	Upgrade technology on a regular basis.
Question:	Is your infrastructure technology good enough to take you into the future? If not, what needs to be added or changed?

15

Implementing Strategic Fluff

G. **Rules:** All organizations have formal and informal ways of operating. Sometimes the workforce pays attention to the "official" way to operate; sometimes they have their own approach. Ideally, policies and procedures are understood, agreed-upon and used in a way to allow new members to "learn the ropes" quickly and efficiently. What can you do with your approach?

	Enforce your policies and procedures and get everyone "on the same page."
	Add needed rules to align your organization
	Drop rules that get in the way of serving customers
	Acknowledge the informal and incorporate it where it makes sense

Question: Do all your rules make sense considering your espoused strategy?

H.   Metrics: What measures and incentives drive actual performance (for better or worse?) Do you have the right key performance indicators (KPIs) to drive your strategy to success?

	Add KPIs that are aligned with your strategic goals.
	Drop KPIs that will trigger behaviors not aligned with your strategic goals.
	Prioritize metrics to focus attention on needed performance.

Question: Do you have so many KPIs as to confuse your managers? What are the most important metrics?

I. **Partners:** Whether paid or not, who helps you run your business? Accountants? Lawyers? Advisors? Coaches? What can you do with partners?

	Keep your existing business partners.
	Drop partners who have become a burden.
	Work with your partners on a joint strategy
	Add new partners
Question: Would you have the same set of business partners if you had to pick them today?	

Implementing Strategic Fluff

I. Resources: Resources are those things you possess (or need to possess) that are converted into products and services. Money, patents, know-how, manufacturing facilities, diagnostic equipment and brand reputation are all examples of needed resources. What might you do about needed and existing resources?

	Acquire needed resources. (e.g., IPO for money. R&D for know-how. Acquisitions for biotech talent.)
	Sell unnecessary resources. (e.g., Business unit spin-off.)
	Develop proprietary resources (e.g., intellectual property)
Questions:	What resources will you need that you don't have now? What resources need to be eliminated?

A PROBLEM TO CONSIDER AND RESOLVE

This list seems rather straight-forward but there is a problem in all organizations – the decision rights to these factors generally lie within functional boundaries (aka, silos).

For example, changes to customers and consumers are generally handled by marketing and sales. Location is often under the auspices of "development." Infrastructure Technology is generally managed by Information Technology. And so on.

Strategy may require changes that are outside of your control. That does not let you off the hook – accept the responsibility to influence other decision makers for the good of the organization.

WARNING: Make sure your strategic thinking is always cross-functional. If you cannot make needed changes, your job is to influence those who can.

Implementing Strategic Fluff

STRATEGY FACTORS MATRIX

The following graphic shows all twelve of the factors that affect your strategy and the potential set of sixty-six 1:1 interrelationships. It looks confusing, but each cell to the right is simply a combination of two factors. A good deal of the job of implementing high-level strategy is considering a change to one factor and how this change impacts the other factors.

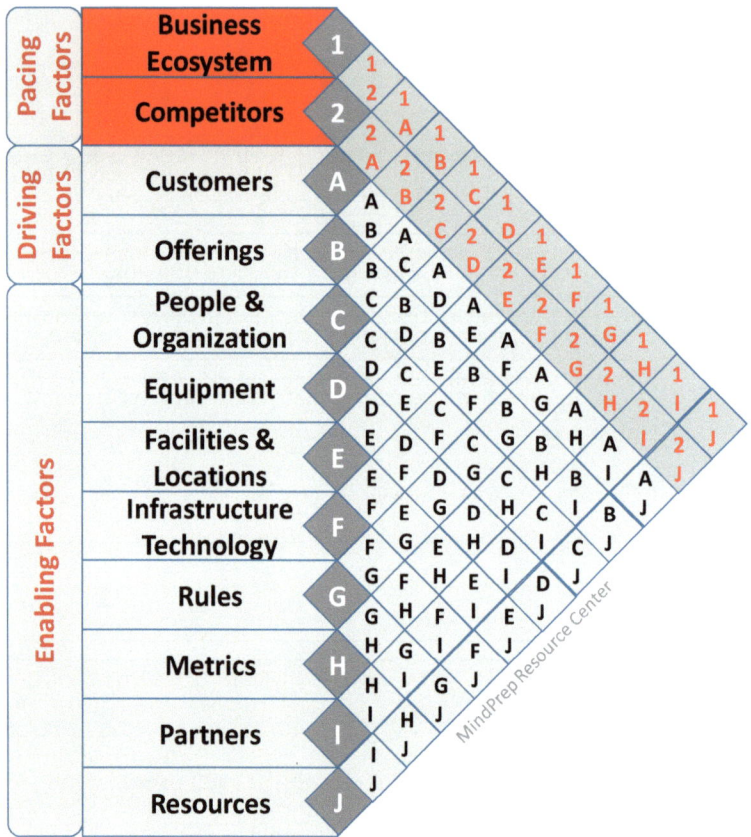

Business Ecosystem and Competitor factors signal the big picture of competition and set the pace for strategic change. The remaining ten factors are then changed and aligned to make your overall strategy coherent. Customers and offerings should drive changes in the eight enabling factors.

Start by considering each of the factors independent of one another. What is changing around you and what do you have to do to respond?

Implementing Strategic Fluff

> Since strategic changes tend to come from the larger environment, start with the Pacing Factors (Business Ecosystem and Competitors) in order to better understand the context for strategic change. As you look around:
>
> - What's new?
>
> - What's changing?
>
> - What's "weird?"
>
> - Where do you sense opportunity?

Now look at the remaining factors and perform a quick SWOT assessment. Given the changes you see, are you changing the right factors? Make this a quick exercise. You will dig deeper in a bit.

> Our strategy will require us to change the following factors and for the following reasons.

STEP 3: GET READY TO WORK CROSS-FUNCTIONALLY:

Now consider the trade-offs that are needed to make the factors work as an integrated whole. The matrix to the right of the factors is the "integration field" that companies must align to get strategy to the point where it can be executed. It's the realm of cross-functional thinking.

I created this list and matrix to help my clients think about strategic decisions in light of decisions being made by others, and to assess the ripple effects of changes in one factor across any or all of the other factors.

The Strategy Factors Matrix is simply a tool to help you organize your thinking as you embark on a big strategic project or wrestle with how to respond to a competitor's move.

Use it as-is or modify it to address your particular circumstances. I've used versions of this graphic to organize the design of a green-field gear manufacturing operation for a major aerospace company and to move a family business from Chicago to Phoenix. I've also used it to organize my thinking when I was on the planning committee for a new hospital.

Although the matrix looks a bit complicated, it's quite simple to read and use:

- Each cell signifies the relationship between two factors. For example, the cell labeled "AG" shows the intersection of Customers and Rules. So, for example, if your strategy requires you to appeal to Gen Z you may have to also think about how you will treat them differently (or not) than you treat Boomers.

- A detailed examination of this matrix follows in Parts 2 and 3.

If you are not willing to think and act cross-functionally you should prepare for failure!

Implementing Strategic Fluff

Once again, here is the factors matrix. Now it's time to dig deeper into the factors and how they impact one another.

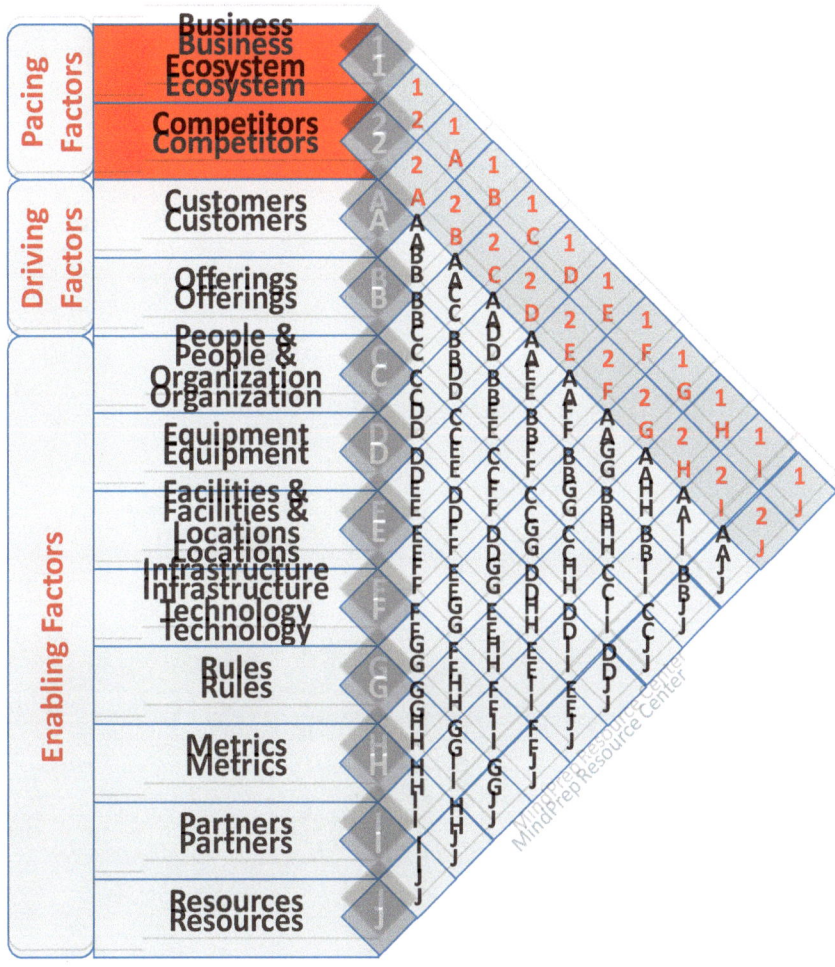

Part 2 of this workbook follows and describes the use of this tool for **business ecosystems and competitor intelligence**.

PART 2: BUSINESS ECOSYSTEM AND COMPETITOR INTELLIGENCE

As you develop and implement strategy for your organization you need to consider a couple of lines of investigation:

- Competitor intelligence – the impact of competitors and their moves across your nine strategic factors; how your competitors are dealing with an evolving ecosystem.

- Business ecosystem analysis – how changes in the business ecology can and will affect your decisions about all the other strategic factors.

STEP 4: THINK ABOUT YOUR BUSINESS ENVIRONMENT

Pacing Factors
- Business Ecosystem
- Competitors

Driving Factors
- Customers
- Offerings

Enabling Factors
- People & Organization
- Equipment
- Facilities & Locations
- Infrastructure Technology
- Rules
- Metrics
- Partners
- Resources

Implementing Strategic Fluff

1. **Business Ecosystem:** Business is long past the "machine" metaphor stage of thinking. Our industries and marketplaces resemble an ecology more than a machine. Like any ecosystem, the reality is that everything affects everything. There is both static and dynamic complexity in play – many parts and all are in motion.

Look around at the business environment in which you operate. What do you see? What words come to mind? (Growing? Dying? Stale? Evolving? Etc.) Describe your ecosystem.

1/2: Competitors in the ecosystem

- Who are your traditional competitors? Are they gaining or losing strength?
- Who has gone out of business and why have they done so?
- Who is entering or about to enter into competition? What might they do differently?

1/A: Customers in the ecosystem

- Who are the buyers of products and services and how are they changing?
- Is loyalty a factor? Was it at one time?
- What are your customers' customers demanding?

Implementing Strategic Fluff

1/B: Products and services in the ecosystem

- Assess the lifecycles of all your offerings. Is this a mature (declining) ecosystem? Look at all the life cycles of your offerings. Where do you see change?

- Where will you get growth?

1/C: People & Organizations in the ecosystem

- Is skilled labor in short supply? Will automation be used to replace / augment people soon?

- How are demographics affecting the supplier, customer and producer bases?

1/D: Resources in the ecosystem

- Are raw materials in short supply? Will they be? (Think global oil industry)

- Who is most innovative? Who uses new knowledge to their advantage? Who has patent protection?

- Whose brand is growing? Whose is declining?

Implementing Strategic Fluff

1/E: Facilities & Locations in the ecosystem

- Has this ecosystem morphed from national to truly global?
- Where is the growth expected? Should you revisit your geography?

1/F: Infrastructure technology in the ecosystem

- What is state of the art and who is using it?
- What is obsolete or rapidly becoming so?
- What's at the edge of your radar screen and moving in fast? (Couldn't resist this!)

1/G: Rules in the ecosystem

- Who has changed the game by changing the way they do business? (Think about Amazon as a retailer.)
- What are customers demanding?
- How will you deal with new or changing customers?

1/H: Metrics in the ecosystem

- How is success measured? Is it the same as it was five years ago? How will future success be measured?

- What defines success for the ecosystem? (Market share? Growth? Profitability? Innovation?)

- Are you measuring new aspects of the ecosystem?

1/J: Partners in the ecosystem

- Have suppliers become competitors to their old customers?

- How are relationships changing?

Implementing Strategic Fluff

STEP 4 (CONT'D): ANSWER THESE QUESTIONS ABOUT YOUR ECOSYSTEM.

1. Given what you see, what are necessary and realistic goals for your organization? Is growth realistic or is survival more of an issue?

2. What needs to change in your organization to take advantage of the changes happening in the ecosystem? Do you have (or can you get) the resources (and enough of them) to achieve your goal?

3. What can you change to align your part of the organization with the overarching goals of the larger organization? If you don't have the needed decision rights, can you influence the real decision makers?

STEP 5: CONSIDER YOUR COMPETITORS.

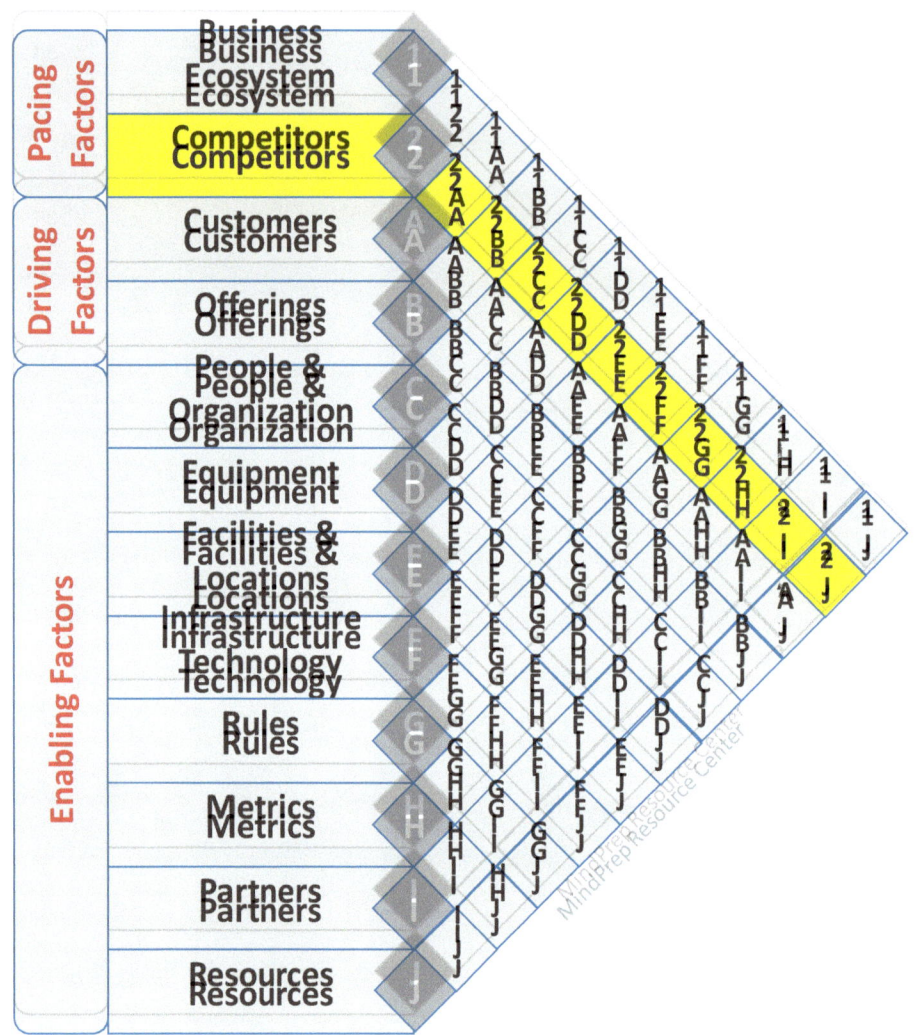

What do you know about your competitors? See if you can answer the general questions I've posed. However, as you consider these questions please realize that you need to ask (and answer) specific questions relating to your company and your competitors.

Implementing Strategic Fluff

2: Competitors

- Who are your current competitors?
- Who are your emerging competitors?
- Who has failed? Why did they fail?
- Who has surprised you with their success?

2/A: Competitors and Customers

- Who buys from whom? Why?
- Why do you lose business? To which competitor(s)?
- Why do you win business?
- What relationship exists between your competitors and customers?

2/B: Competitors and their offerings

- What do they offer and is it better than what you offer?
- Why is it not as good as what you offer?
- Look at your competitors' offerings. What's their value proposition?

Implementing Strategic Fluff

2/C: Competitors, their people and their organization

- How do their best people stack up against your best people?
- Are they organized differently?
- How would you describe their organization's culture?
- Who has a better workforce? Why?

2/D: Competitors and their resources

- Who has the stronger asset base?
- Do they have a knowledge advantage?
- Who has a stronger brand?

2/E: Competitors and locations

- Where are they? Are they real, virtual, or both?
- Are they more convenient to the base of customers?
- Are they in places that surprise you?

Implementing Strategic Fluff

2/F: Competitors and Infrastructure technology

- How do they use social media?
- Are their systems state-of-the-market or state-of-the-art?
- Do their salespeople have better technology for selling?

2/G: Competitors and policies and procedures

- Are they easier to do business with than you?
- How do they acquire talent?
- How do they develop talent?
- Are they more flexible than you?

2/H: Competitors and metrics

- How are their sales people measured?
- How do they measure success? Does this mean organizational success?
- Do they use the same measures as you?

2/I: Competitors and their partners

- Do they have different suppliers than you? Better? Better how?
- Who do they partner with? Why?

STEP 5 (CONT'D): ANSWER THESE QUESTIONS

1. Who serves customers better than you?

2. Who has superior strategic resources?

3. Who's trying to change the game in your industry?

PART 3: THINK CROSS-FUNCTIONALLY

The ten strategic factors that determine your real business strategy correspond, roughly, to the functional areas within your organization.

- Customers >>> marketing and sales
- Offerings >>> marketing & engineering
- People and Organization >>> human resources & C-suite
- Equipment >>> Engineering, operations
- Facilities & Location >>> C-suite, supply chain, operations
- Infrastructure technology >>> IT
- Rules >>> finance, HR, C-suite
- Metrics >>> Operations, HR, finance
- Partners >>> supply chain
- Resources >>> finance

The problem arises when decisions are made in one of the factors without considering the ripple effect across other factors.

Oftentimes great strategic intention falls prey to shortfalls in execution because we fail to "mind the gap."

For example, the installation of a great piece of infrastructure technology falls short of actual implementation because insufficient funds were allocated to training the users. Why? Because the "training dollars" were assumed to be coming from Operations budget. But no one brought Operation into the plan. Both sides pay attention to their "boundaries" but neither side assumes responsibility for the gap between them.

Call it integration or call it cross-functional thinking, the reality is that after all of these years of complaining about "silos," they still exist.

Implementing Strategic Fluff

STEP 6: CONSIDER ALL THE INTERACTIONS AND NECESSARY CHANGES

There are ten strategic factors that are combined to create your strategy. This results in forty-five potential pairs that should be considered as you plan to execute your organization's high-level strategy.

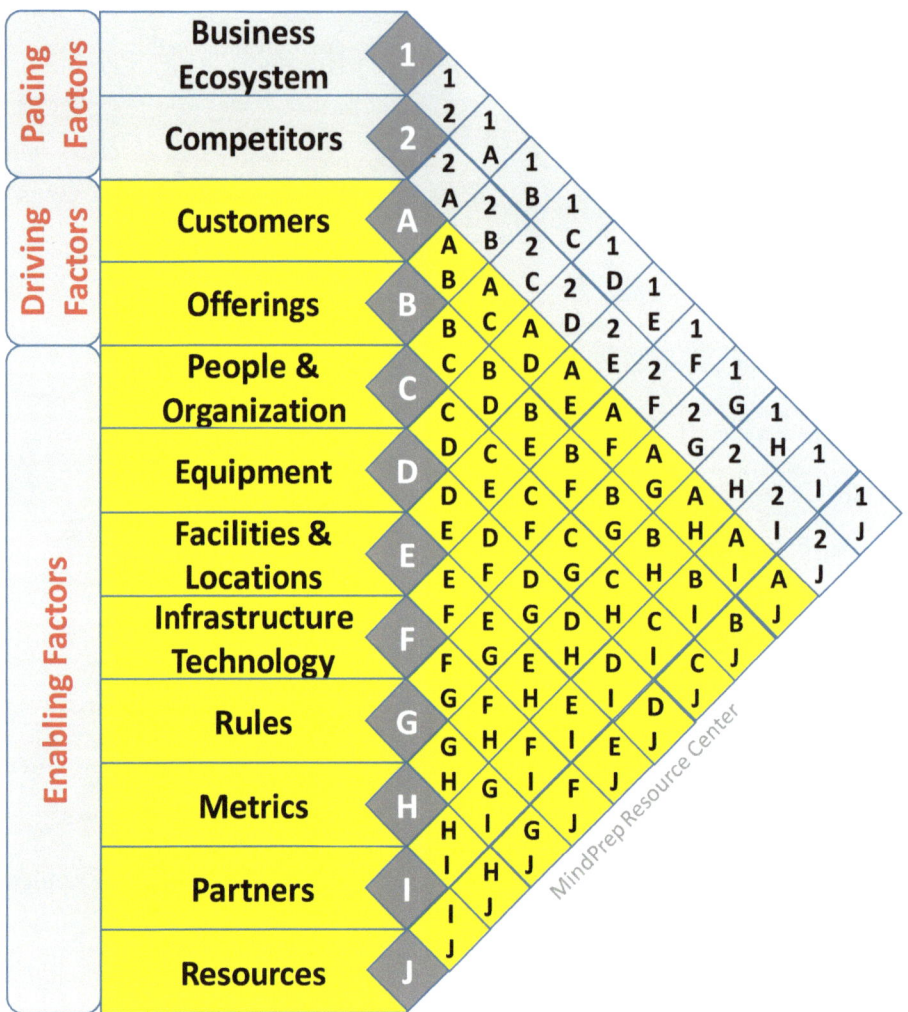

If you change one of the factors to implement your strategy you will always see "ripples" across other factors. You MUST spend time looking for these ripples and figure out what might change and what else must change.

Not spending time doing this dangerous! Don't create strategic holes to fall into.

Implementing Strategic Fluff

ONE ON ONE RELATIONSHIPS

You may be tempted to consider strategic changes only through the lens of your department or function. However, doing so creates "strategic cracks" that are usually discovered during implementation. Look for cracks before you fall into them.

Here are some questions about the relationships between factors that you might want to answer. Once again, I've left space for your insights and questions.

Be prepared to use these insights to answer a few questions are the end of Part 3.

AB – Customers & Offerings

- What do they want that you don't have?
- What did they want? Do they still want it?

AC – Customers & People/Organization

- Do customer-facing workers know what the customers want?
- How much and what kind of communication do the customers want?

Implementing Strategic Fluff

AD – Customers & Equipment

- Do customer requirements for quality and precision exceed the capabilities of your equipment?
- Are there customer requirements that cannot be satisfied with existing equipment?

AE – Customers & Facilities/Location

- Are your locations convenient?
- Do customers care where you are located or do they want to migrate to on-line?

AF – Customers & Infrastructure Technology

- Does your phone system drive customers crazy?
- Is your website up-to-date and easy to navigate?

Implementing Strategic Fluff

AG = Customers & Rules

- Are you easy to do business with?
- What policies anger your customers?

AH = Customers and Metrics

- How do you measure your customers?
- How do customers measure your performance?

AI = Customers & Partners

- Do your business partners understand your customers' needs?
- Would your customers rather go around you to your suppliers?
- Can your partners help with customer retention?

Implementing Strategic Fluff

AJ – Customers & Resources

- How relevant is your brand to the next generation of customers?
- Do your customers feel you treat them well?

BC – Offerings & People / Organization

- Are your people properly trained to produce quality offerings in an effective and efficient manner?
- Are your offerings dangerous to your workers?

BD – Offerings & Equipment

- Do you need different equipment for new offerings?
- Do you have enough capacity? Excess capacity?

Implementing Strategic Fluff

BE – Offerings & Facilities/Location

- Should you offshore? Onshore?
- Do your locations help or hinder supply chain efficiency?

BF – Offerings & Infrastructure Technology

- How good are your production systems?
- How good are your supply chain systems?

BG – Offerings & Rules

- Do you support your offerings?
- Can customers easily make suggestions for improvement?

Implementing Strategic Fluff

BH – Offerings & Metrics

- How do you measure the market success of each offering?
- How do you measure offering quality?

BI – Offerings & Partners

- Whose input is critical to the success of your offering?
- Could the failure of a supplier bring your business to a halt?

BJ – Offerings & Resources

- Do new offerings fit your brand image?
- Is your market information timely enough?

Implementing Strategic Fluff

CD = People / Organization & Equipment

- Do we need to upskill the workforce for new equipment?
- Can the maintenance staff make needed repairs to new equipment?

CE = People / Organization & Facilities/Location

- Should the workforce telecommute?
- Do your locations attract the best talent?

CF = People / Organization & Infrastructure Technology

- Do workers have the right / best IT equipment?
- Is employee data secure?

Implementing Strategic Fluff

CG – People / Organization & Rules

- Is talent development ad hoc or organized?
- Is the performance development system respected by the workforce?

CH -- People / Organization & Metrics

- How do you measure performance?
- Is compensation equitable, defensible, and explainable?

CI – People / Organization & Partners

- Do you know key partner personnel?
- Do you let employees make "field trips" to key partners?

Implementing Strategic Fluff

CJ – People / Organization & Resources

- What tools do your workers need to be (more) productive?
- Are department budgets allocated according to value received?

DE – Equipment & Facilities/Location

- Is the equipment layout conducive to smooth flow and material and people?
- Can the facility handle the heating and cooling needs of the equipment and its operators?

DF -- Equipment & Infrastructure Technology

- Can the facility handle wired and wireless communication?
- Is space allocated for networking / copying / testing equipment

Implementing Strategic Fluff

DG -- Equipment & Rules

- Are safety rules posted and accessible?
- Have preventive and predictive procedures been vetted?

DH -- Equipment & Metrics

- Have uptime and throughput requirements been set and are they measured?
- Are sources of downtime tracked and evaluated?

DI -- Equipment & Partners

- Do you consider your vendors to be business partners? If not, why not?
- Do you avail yourself of vendor training?

Implementing Strategic Fluff

DJ = Equipment & Resources

- What is your budget for preventive and predictive maintenance?
- Have you considered special purpose equipment that might give you a competitive advantage?

EF = Facilities/Location & Infrastructure Technology

- How secure is your data back-up site?
- Are your operations and your IT development team co-located?

EG = Facilities/Location & Rules

- Are all locations treated the same or does HQ get a better deal? (Ask the folks in the field.)
- Are all your "time zones" treated fairly?

Implementing Strategic Fluff

EH – Facilities/Location & Metrics

- Are measurement systems localized or global?
- Do distant managers feel cheated or relieved because of the distance from HQ?

EI – Facilities/Location & Partners

- What cultural obstacles exist across the span of your global partners?
- Can your partners match your global reach?

EJ – Facilities/Location & Resources

- Are your locations where your customers want them?
- Do you need to open or close a territory?

Implementing Strategic Fluff

FG – Infrastructure Technology & Rules

- Is system efficiency degraded because of the need for workarounds?
- Are your policies and procedures responsive to the flood of data hitting your systems?

FH – Infrastructure Technology & Metrics

- How do you measure the impact of new technology?
- Do existing metrics prevent taking a risk with new technology?

FI – Infrastructure Technology & Partners

- Are you and your partners working in silos or have you integrated your technologies?
- What information is needed by your partners? Do they get it in a timely manner?

Implementing Strategic Fluff

FJ – Infrastructure Technology & Resources

- Have you devoted enough money to fund the infrastructure you will need in the coming five years?
- What is/will be obsolete and what are you going to do about it?

GH – Rules & Metrics

- Are your policies and procedures efficient?
- Are they effective?

GI – Rules & Partners

- In what ways do you and your partners disagree?
- How do you resolve these disagreements?

Implementing Strategic Fluff

GJ = Rules & Resources

- Is the logic of resource development a "corporate secret?"
- Is your brand supported by the action of the front-line workers?

HI = Metrics & Partners

- How do you measure the working success of your partners?
- How do they measure working with you?

HJ = Metrics & Resources

- Do you measure the ROI of brand development?
- What metrics make you nervous? Are important metrics missing?

IJ = Resources & Partners

- Do your partners supply intellectual capital to your business?
- How do your partners share the risk inherent in your strategy?

STEP 6 (CONT'D): ANSWER THESE QUESTIONS

Given our espoused strategy and what we know about competitors and our ecosystem, what should we change?

Given our resources and attitudes, what <u>can</u> we change?

Considering the ripple effect of change, what else will change or will have to change?

Implementing Strategic Fluff

PART 4: BRINGING IT ALL TOGETHER

STEP 7: SUMMARIZE THE SITUATION

In order to keep up with the pace of industry evolution you need five capabilities. You need to be able to:

- **Understand the real values, vision and goals of your organization.** These are the elements that align an organization. Without a common understanding and acceptance of them you will most likely have groups working at cross purposes.

> Talk with your boss. What are you trying to accomplish? What does she value?

- **Sense the signals of existing and emerging challenges.** The future is NOT a straight-line extension of the past. If you miss the signals of change you risk becoming irrelevant to your customers, consumers and stakeholders.

> What are the most important changes you see with your competitors and business ecosystem? How are they changing your company's strategy?

Implementing Strategic Fluff

- **Make sense of what you perceive.** Now, take some time to really think hard about the following:

What is your company's strategy trying to accomplish? What does success look like?

What assumptions are you making about the strategy and your ability to execute it?

Have you considered which of the factors need to change? Have you discussed alternatives?

Implementing Strategic Fluff

8. **Decide on a course of action.** Thinking is interesting; but decision-making is the heart of leadership. And if you are not in a position of making key decisions you are not excused. It then becomes your responsibility to influence decision-makers for the good of your organization.

Which of the strategy factors will you change? Which of the factors are you not allowed to change (or are afraid to change)? Use the following checklist to get a picture of the challenge ahead of you:

FACTORS	SHOULD CHANGE	CAN CHANGE	WILL CHANGE
CUSTOMER OFFERINGS			
PEOPLE & ORGANIZATION			
EQUIPMENT			
FACILITIES & LOCATIONS			
INFRASTRUCTURE TECHNOLOGY			
RULES			
METRICS			
PARTNERS			
RESOURCES			

Implementing Strategic Fluff

Act on your decisions. Executing on your decisions brings espoused strategy to reality. There is always a gap between intention and execution. Your job is to minimize the gap.

What capabilities will you need that you don't have now? How will you acquire them?

Do you have the capacity to do what you need to do?

STEP 8: THINK LIKE A PROJECT / PROGRAM LEADER

Strategy always results in a portfolio of projects and programs that have to be executed at the same time. Furthermore, you are likely to be an "accidental project manager" with a "day job" to manage while you also deal with the triple constrains of time, money and scope.

Your options at this point are to either find some great project managers or to take a crash course in project management and hope for the best.

PROJECT LEADERSHIP CHECKLIST

It's beyond the scope of this workshop and workbook to go into the detail of managing strategic projects. That said, use the Project Readiness Assessment that follows to consider the decisions that have to be made to increase the odds of success.

Stay as far to the left as possible. Scores on the right will signal problems with turning strategy into reality.

OK, now go and make strategy real for your organization. Enjoy the adventure

Implementing Strategic Fluff

CATEGORIES	Ideal	Neutral		Project killer
Requirements	Statement of work is complete and signed by the project client.	Statement of work is complete, and the client has given verbal agreement	The project has been discussed with the client; however, little has been put in writing	The statement of work has been set by the management team; users have not been consulted	There is no statement of work. Deliverables have been identified, but not detailed.
Sponsorship	Project sponsors will use the deliverable and willingly provide the project budget.	Project sponsors agree to use the deliverable; funding is provided from a corporate account.	Sponsors are indifferent regarding success or failure; funding is provided from a corporate account.	Sponsors see the project as "nice" but have other uses for their constrained budget.	An executive has been told that she will provide the budget for the project and sees the project as an intrusion
Team (quantity and skills)	Team is qualified and already assigned to the project. This will be their sole project.	Team is qualified and this is their primary project. They have minor demands on their time for other duties.	Team is qualified and this is their primary project. However, this is a virtual team	The team is marginally qualified; they have been assigned because they have the available time.	The team has not been identified; all members will have regular work duties in addition to this project.
Budget	This project has a budget that is sufficient and dedicated. Budget is controlled by the PM.	This project has an initial budget that is sufficient and dedicated but controlled by functional management.	This project comes under an umbrella project and will have to compete for resources	This project has a budget that was based on available resources and rough estimates of needs.	This project will have to rely on existing operating funds. The project does not have its own budget.
Project Leadership	The assigned project leader has the right experience and wants to work on this project	The assigned project leader has significant complementary experience and wants to work on this project.	The assigned project leader has little complementary experience and wants to work on this project.	The assigned project leader was chosen because he/she was available but has other duties as well	The assigned project leader has other duties and does not want to work on this project.

CATEGORIES	Ideal	Neutral	Project Killer
Business needs	This project is considered fundamental to the success of the organization's business strategy by the entire organization	This project is seen as important by the leadership team but has not been widely acknowledged	This project is seen as "nice to make a jibe" but is not seen as necessary.	Senior stakeholders are opposed to using company time and resources for this project.
Organization's project culture	This organization has a culture of successful project and that is using policies and procedures for conducting projects	Project are seen as important but there is no consistent but extra effort and time.	Projects are seen as important but as additional, non-compensated work.	Past projects have resulted in minor or no stakeholders. There are powerful stakeholders opposed to this project. Projects are seen as the gravely of future careers that have no future.
Planning and scheduling	The entire project team was involved in the planning process. The deadlines seem reasonable.	A project plan was created and reviewed with the core team and final plan was presented to the team. Important changes are made to the plan.	A project plan was developed by the core team and presented to the team.	A project plan is discussed but a full plan was not developed and documented.	No project plan exists. Deadlines are set by management who are explained to the team.
Portfolio of projects	The organization has an active project management office (PMO) and this project has been included in the portfolio of projects	The organization has an active PMO, however, this project has not yet been included in the portfolio of projects	All major projects are reviewed regularly by the executive for cross functional alignment and requirements are explained.	Projects are developed within functional silos and compete for resources and talent within the functional areas.	All projects exist and are not compared for resources and talent.
Change Control	Change control processes exist and are used throughout the organization. Tradeoffs are made as changes arise.	Changes are formally handled within the team. Tradeoffs are discussed and it trigger replanning of the project.	Changes are handled on an ad hoc basis by the project team. Tradeoffs are brought to senior management as a last resort.	Changes are handled on an ad hoc basis by the project team. Tradeoffs are discussed and considered.	Senior management will not consider changes to deadlines, scope, or budget.

BILL WELTER

Bill is a consulting-educator with over 50 years of experience spanning four separate careers: military, engineering, consulting and education.

He's a founding Principal of MindPrep Resource Center, a small business that specializes in helping business leaders and professionals become better thinkers and leaders. He does this through writing, speeches, workshops, team facilitation, and one-on-one coaching.

Bill has written five books.

- He is the lead co-author of *The Prepared Mind of a Leader: Eight Skills Leaders Use to Innovate, Make Decisions, and Solve Problems* (Jossey-Bass, 2006).
- He co-authored *Rethink, Reinvent, Reposition: 12 Strategies to Renew Your Business* (Adams Media, 2010).
- He authored an e-book for Adams Media in 2011: *Rightsizing Your Business: Breakthrough Strategies to Create a Flexible and Profitable Business in Any Economy*
- *MindLab It*, was published in 2014 to provide short exercises to improve critical thinking.
- *Demystifying Business Strategy* was published in 2019. This concise workbook is focused on helping leaders answer six questions that demand solid answers.

Contact: Telephone: (312) 802-6476 or bill.welter@mindprep.com. Offices are in Loveland, Colorado.

www.ingramcontent.com/pod-product-compliance
Lightning Source LLC
Chambersburg PA
CBHW051919210526
45473CB00006B/2068